STEAL THEIR STYLE!

Meet the models and read about their fabulous outfits! You can use our fashion tips and styles to inspire your own designs later in the book.

Tabitha

Likes:
High heels

Dislikes:
Chunky jewelry

Fashion Style:
Classy

Grace

Likes:
Performing

Dislikes:
Football

Fashion Style:
Daring

This emerald green dress looks sensational on Tabitha, and her shoes match perfectly with the gold detailing on the neckline.

The bold and busy pattern on Grace's dress really suits her edgy look! A timeless bowling bag finishes off this outfit.

SUPER SPARKLES

Carly
Likes:
Chocolate
Dislikes:
Ironing
Fashion Style:
Showy

Rosie
Likes:
Pancakes
Dislikes:
Thunder storms
Fashion Style:
Dainty

Rosie looks like a fairytale princess in this layered light pink dress. The sparkly accessories and shoes bring the outfit together perfectly.

Carly is looking unquestionably sophisticated in this ensemble! The hot pink skirt and sparkling gold top create a punchy vibe with minimal effort.

When the occasion is right, bring out the shimmer! Nothing makes a bolder statement than a bit of glitz. Sequins can be used to add glamour to an everyday outfit or when creating a dress to dazzle!

Sienna

Likes:
Jogging

Dislikes:
Ghost stories

Fashion Style:
Perky

Sienna is stunning in this turquoise one-shoulder mini-dress! The belt and neckline detail add interest and the bold shoes give a splash of color.

Isabel

Likes:
Formal occasions

Dislikes:
Shellfish

Fashion Style:
Tailored

Isabel is sure to turn heads in this striking black dress. Her shoes match the outfit to perfection and the purple blazer gives it a professional twist!

COUNTRYSIDE CHIC

Heather
Likes:
Hats
Dislikes:
Serious suits
Fashion Style:
Easygoing

Frances
Likes:
Dancing
Dislikes:
Swimming
Fashion Style:
Spirited

Nipping in at the waist, this dress is fantastically flattering on Heather. Her fedora hat and long black boots give it a fun country edge.

This long green jacket instantly adds a country feel to this outfit. The heeled buckle boots with an open-toe design makes this look downright chic!

Casual attire is a "must have" in any wardrobe. Just because it's practical and comfortable, it doesn't have to be boring! Keep it fun, stylish, and cool by adding some countryside accessories.

George
Likes:
Hamburgers
Dislikes:
Being indoors
Fashion Style:
Laid-back

A traditional plaid shirt, paired with blue jeans, is a classic combination! This easygoing look is ideal for any day of the week.

Sienna's busy flower print t-shirt creates an awesome contrast when teamed with her pale blue jeans! A classic brown satchel and comfy pink shoes make this look totally practical.

LOVELY LACE

Wow! This figure-hugging lace dress looks amazing on Kiara. The bright blue makes a bold statement, and the chunky rings add an edge to this unique style.

Isabel pairs this lace jacket with matching ankle boots to turn a daytime outfit into a stylish evening ensemble.

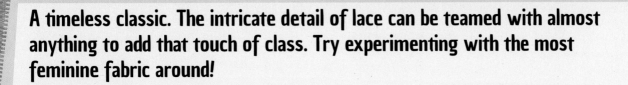

A timeless classic. The intricate detail of lace can be teamed with almost anything to add that touch of class. Try experimenting with the most feminine fabric around!

Black lace looks truly striking when teamed with a bold base layer. Carly's dress shows the intricacy and fine detail of the lace to its best effect.

Taking a classic fabric like ivory lace and making it into a modern dress is just so cool. Rosie teams the dress with a bold purple belt and rugged brown boots.

POWER PATTERNS

Orlando
Likes:
Social events
Dislikes:
Bats
Fashion Style:
Smart cool

Orlando is truly working this preppy polo shirt! The green really pops against the earthy neutral shades in his pants and shoes.

Grace looks stunning in this long skirt with a bright floral pattern. The dark blue tone from the skirt is used for her top, and a pair of classic black heels completes the look.

By wearing bold patterns, you'll make a powerful fashion statement. Take care when mixing your patterns—classic looks combine a bold statement pattern with a plain stylish garment.

With these patterned jeans, Carly adds an element of worn retro chic to her outfit. Experiment with using different prints on your skinny jean designs.

Animal prints are always funky and daring! Kiara's pants will definitely cause a stir. Matching them with a bright orange top really sets off the black and white print.

SPORT STYLE

Tabitha is looking totally trim in her gym gear, yet it's 100% practical. Pairing bright colors with a plain base is a winner!

Bold and funky colors ensure a fresh look for George on the slopes. Experiment with bold shapes on your snowboarding and skiing gear.

Whoever said sport and style don't go together? Coordinate your separate sports items by wearing complimentary colors and matching your accessories. Sportswear never looked so stylish!

Tennis dresses aren't just for the court. Sienna teams hers with white wedge sneakers to sharpen this playful look.

Looking relaxed in her matching sports gear, Isabel is ready for her yoga class. Wearing comfortable leggings and a bright sports top, she's all about style!

PRETTY PASTELS

Grace's floaty summer dress in this pastel green could be dressed up or down depending on the accessories. Think about the occasion before creating your outfit.

Rosie is looking simply adorable in this spotty dress! The blue wedges and pink headband with bow detail complete the look.

Life is sweet with these sugary shades of green, pink, yellow, and blue. Shed those heavy winter tones and step into spring wearing something from a pretty pastel palette!

Casual and cool in her lemon maxi skirt, Heather shows that this daytime look is absolutely wearable and stylish. Add bright bangles to make the look zing!

Layering up using similar tones accomplishes a trendy, yet practical effect. Frances is a serious trendsetter in this sweet summer styling.

CITY SLICKERS

Frances really means business in her wet-look leggings and fantastic fitted blazer! The look is softened by the purple peep-toe platform shoes with bow detail.

Create impact by making your model's dress a bright, solid shade. Grace really stands out in her orange cap sleeve dress and strappy black heels.

Rock that big city vibe and become a real urban trendsetter—where stylish meets serious. Team together sharp classics, such as fitted vests and blazers, with bold shades to create a real impact.

Wearing a smart vest, yellow shirt, and tie, Orlando is checking all the boxes! Team these items with jeans to create a great smart casual look.

Tabitha is keeping warm in rich berry tones and thick woolen tights. Her green purse gives this look a daytime slant while keeping it chic.

START DESIGNING!

Time to create your own collection! Start by penciling in the shape of your clothing over the figure outline, then add color, pattern, and style!

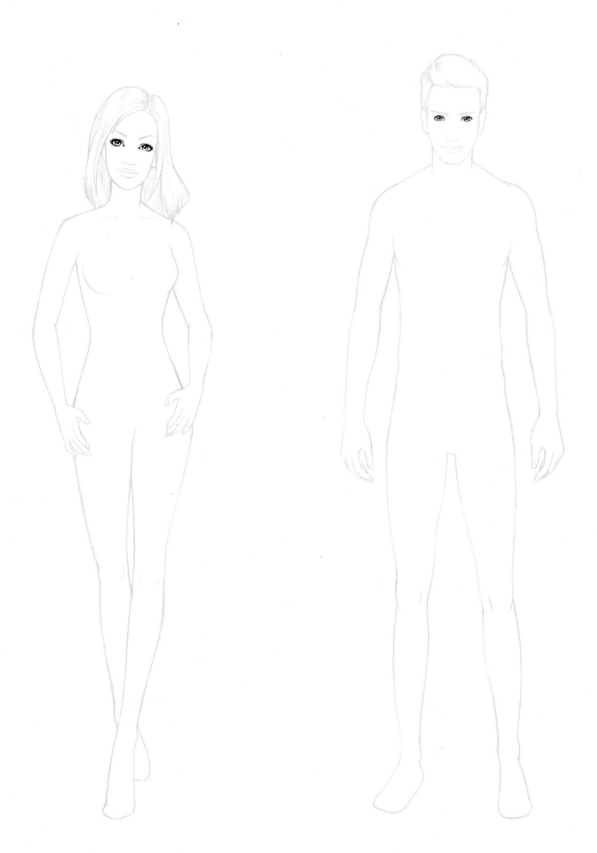

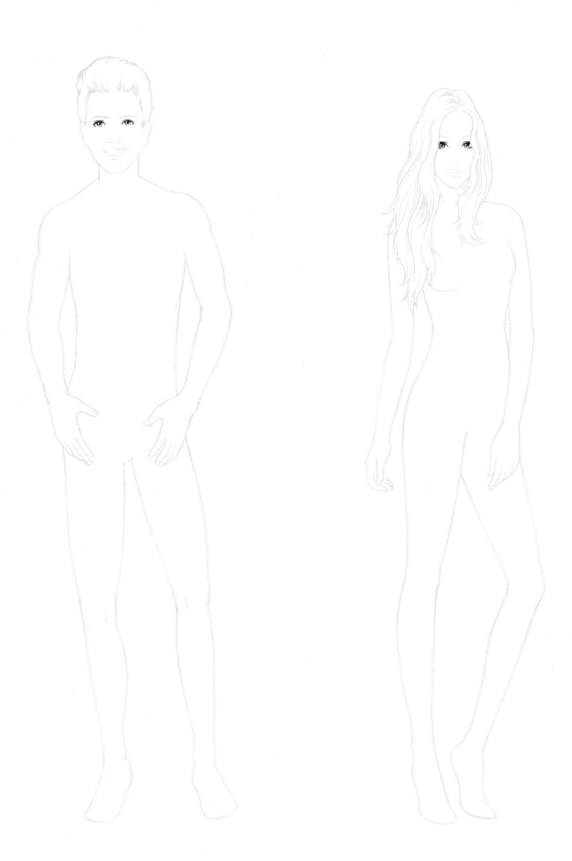

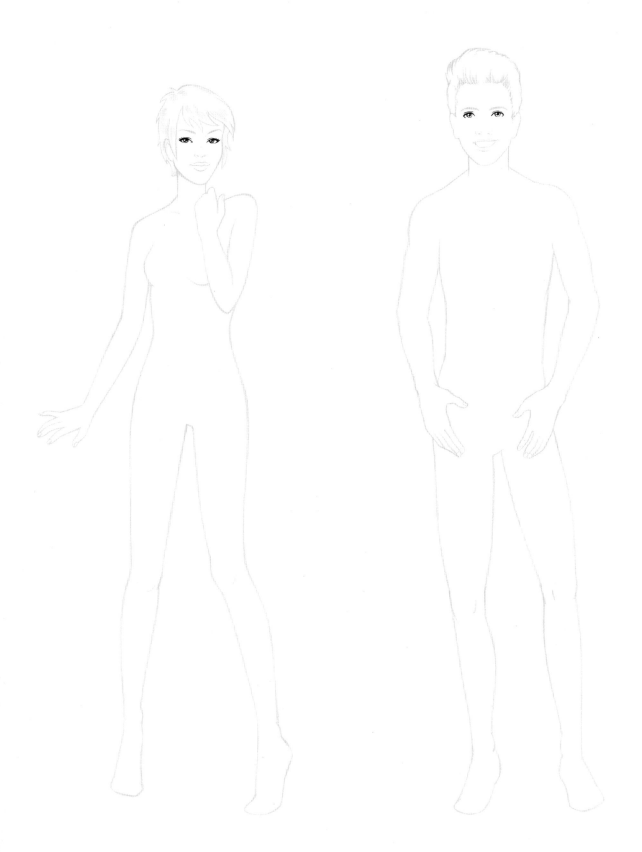

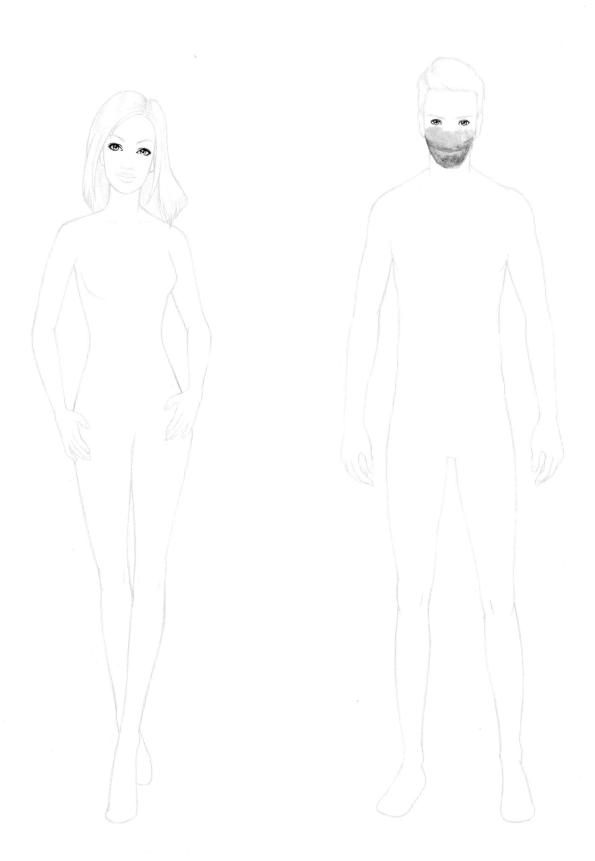

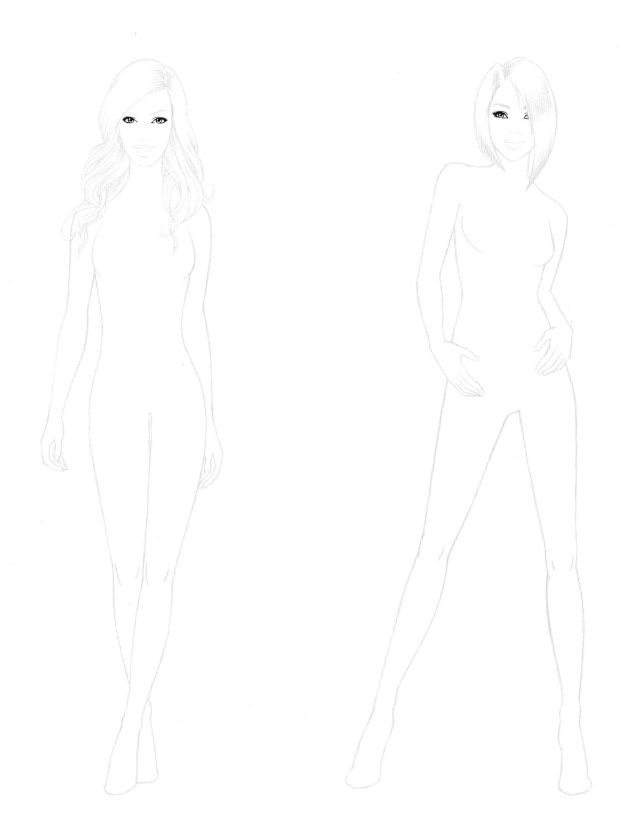

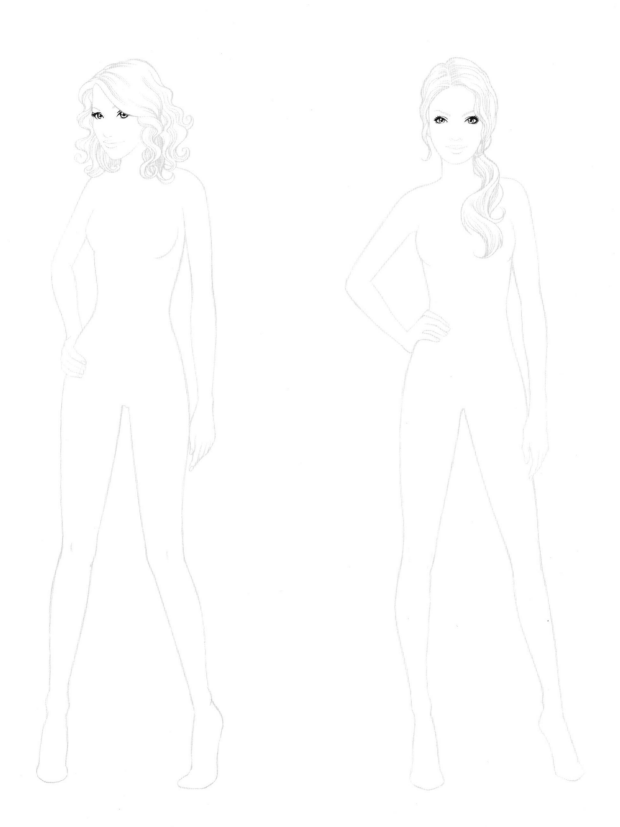

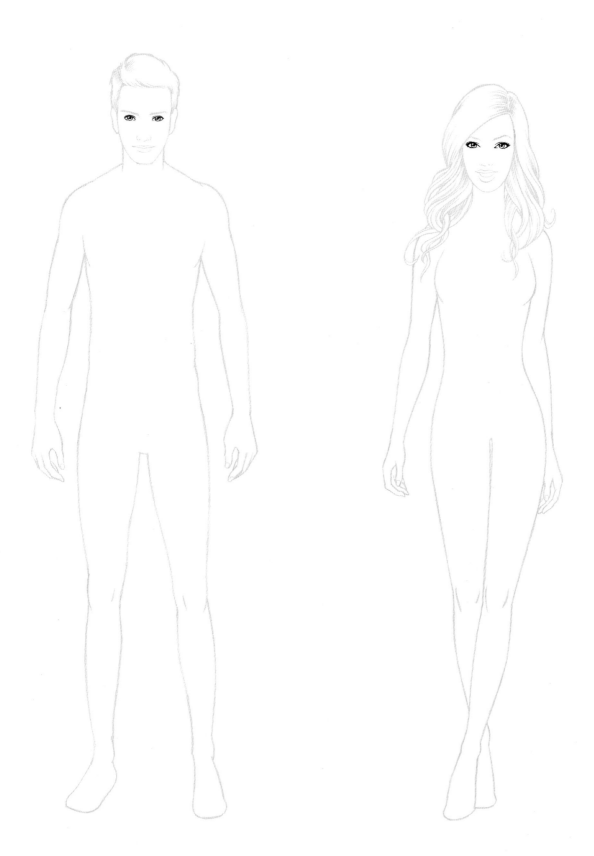

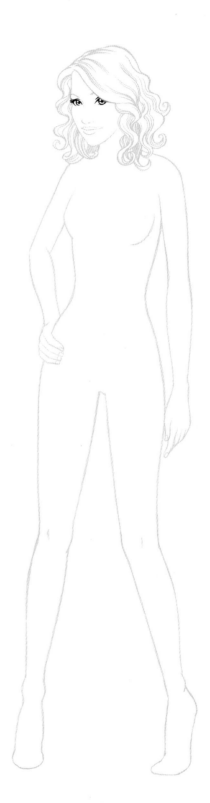

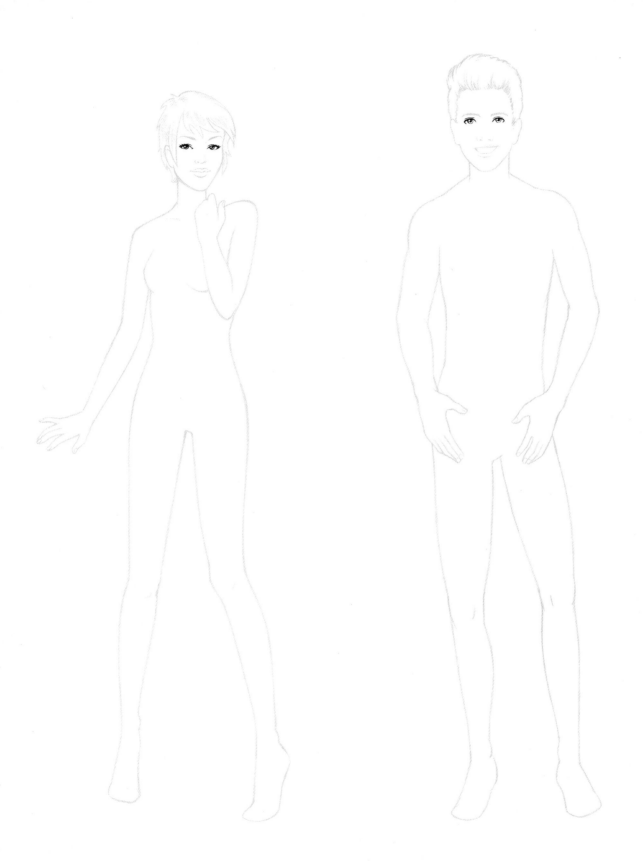

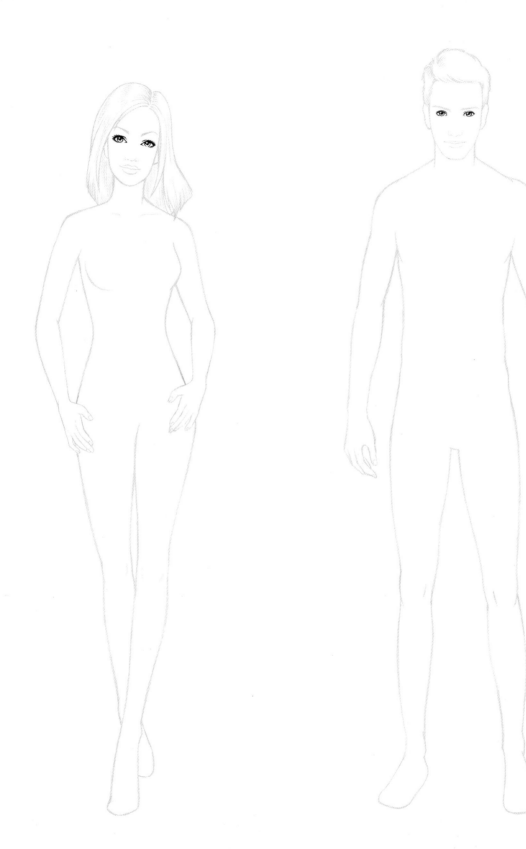

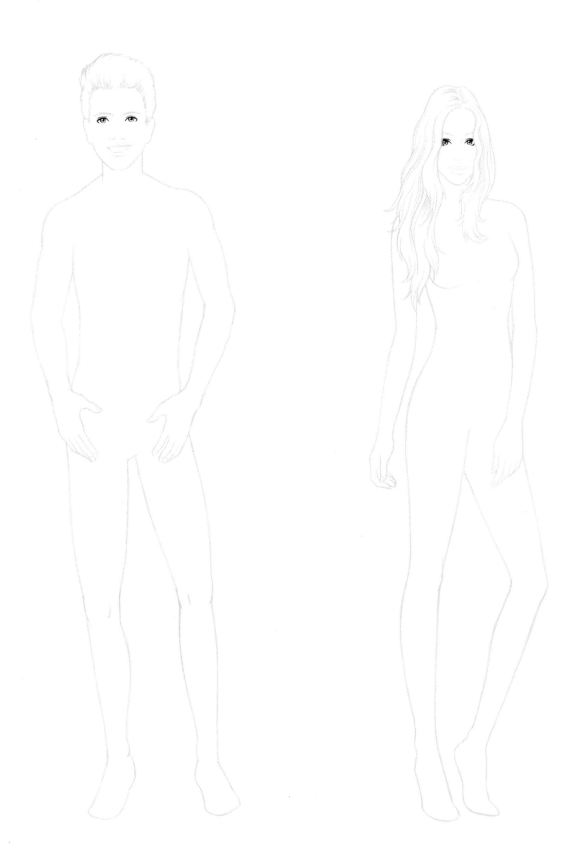

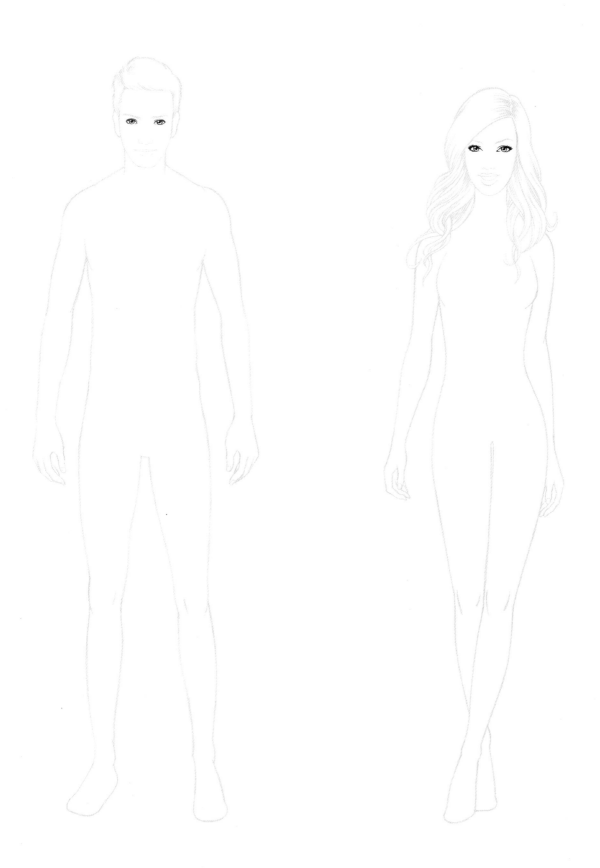

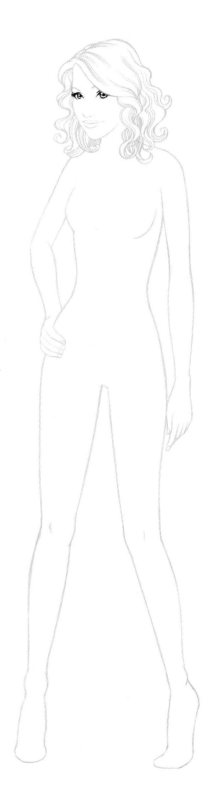

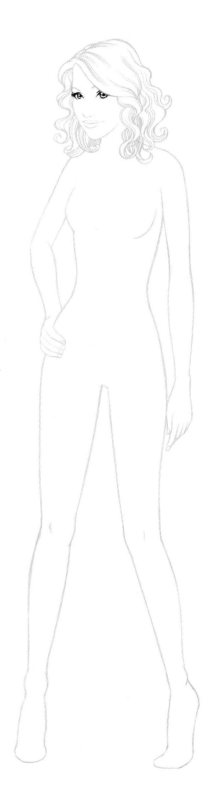

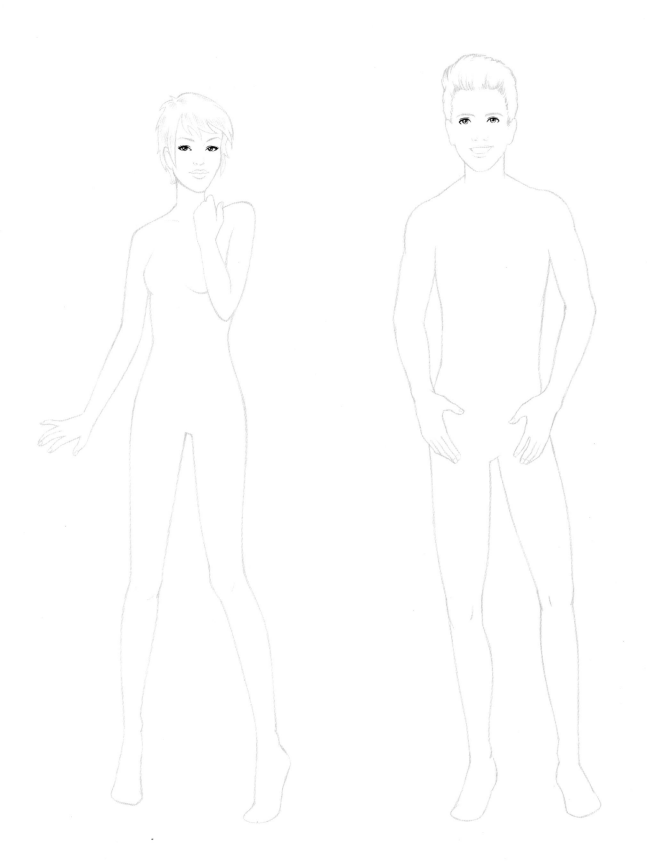

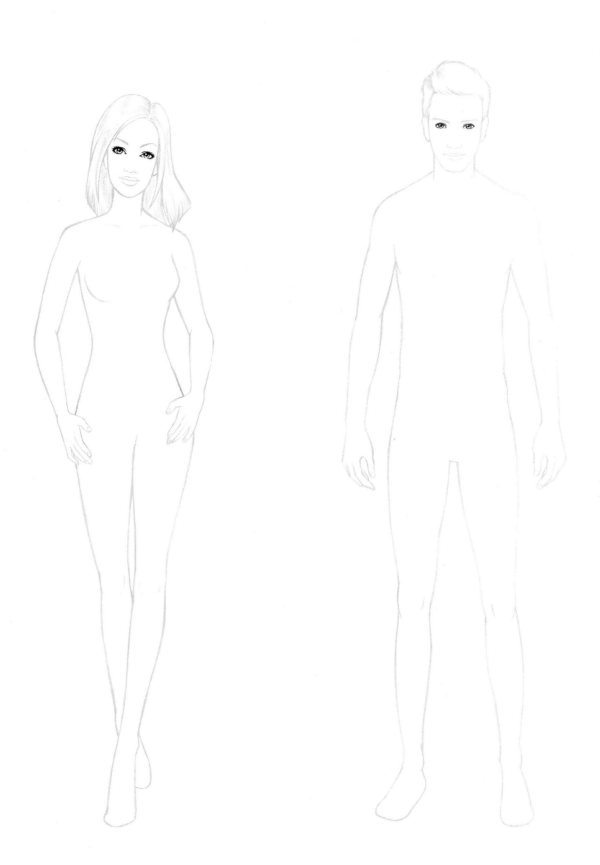

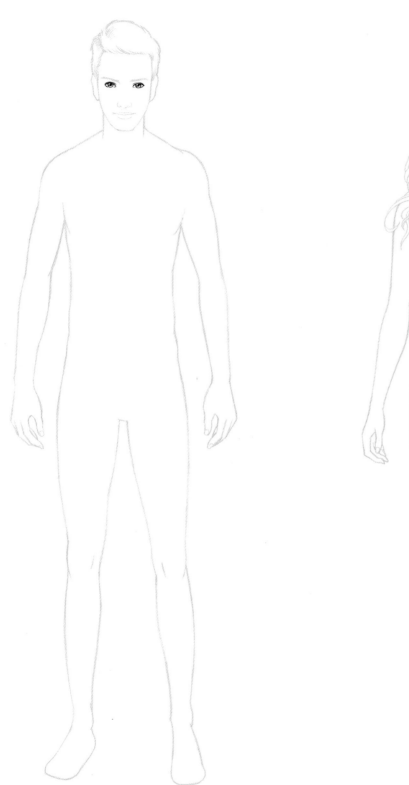
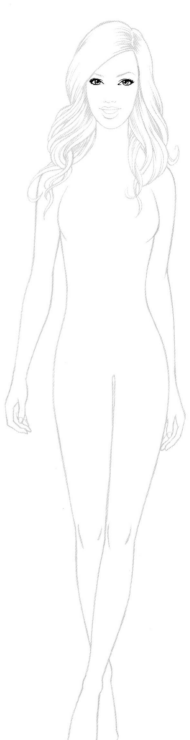

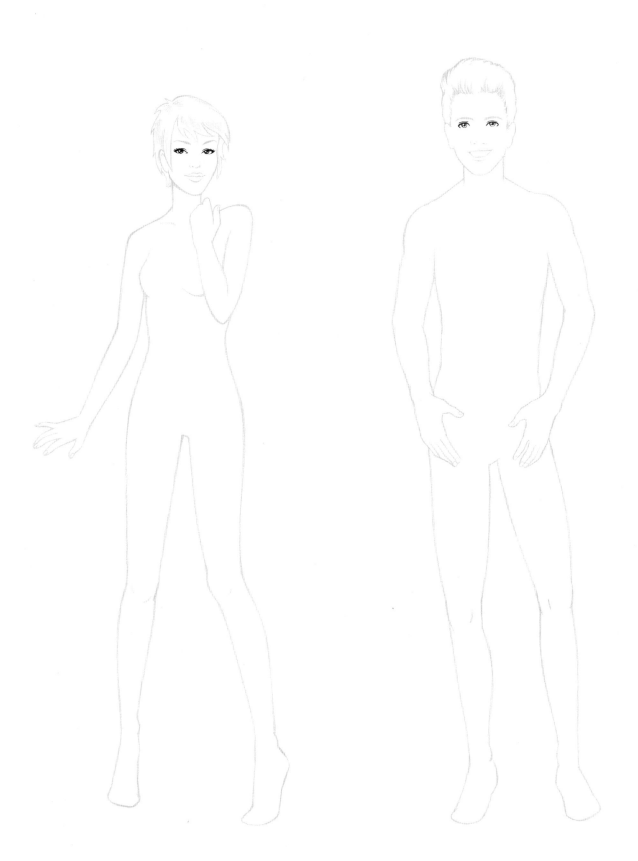

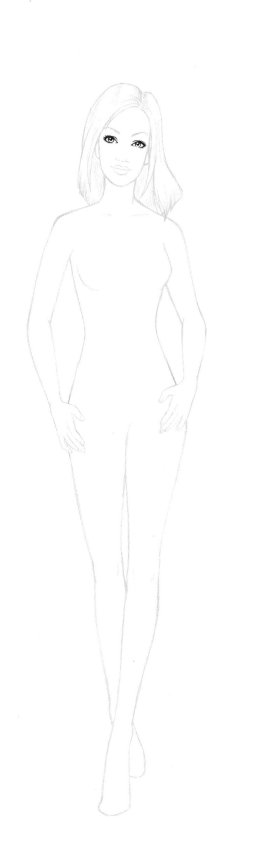
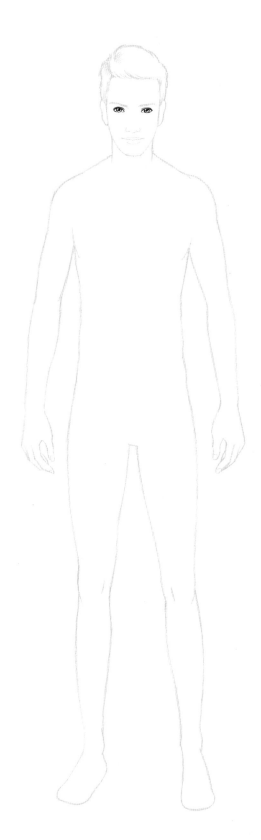

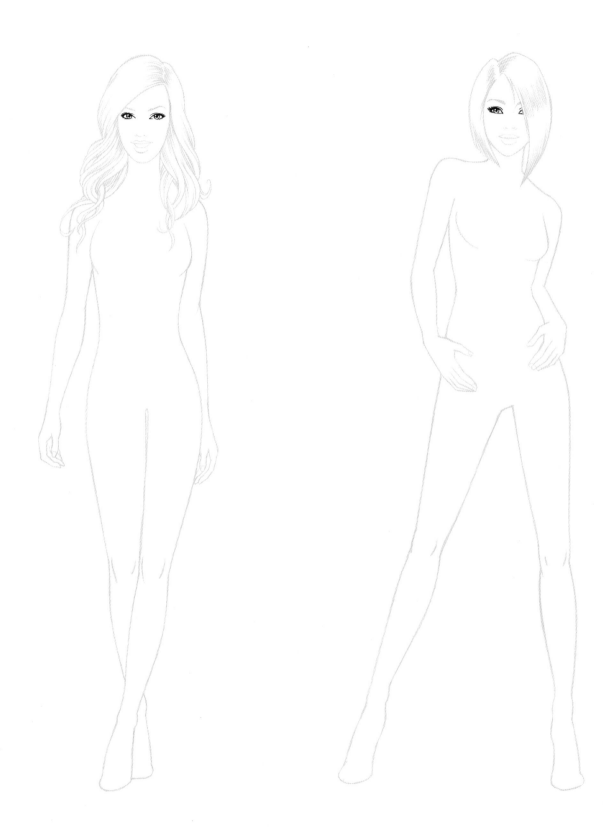

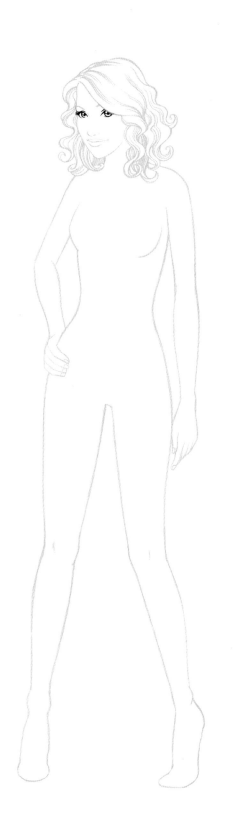

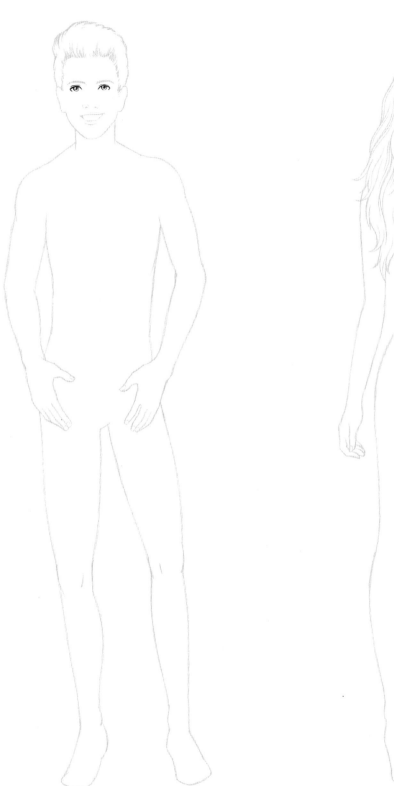
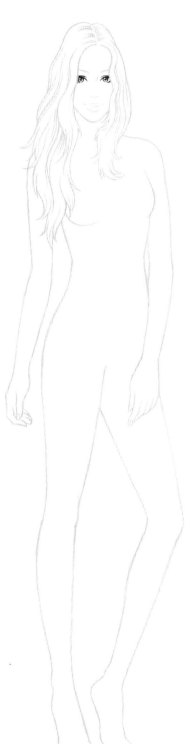

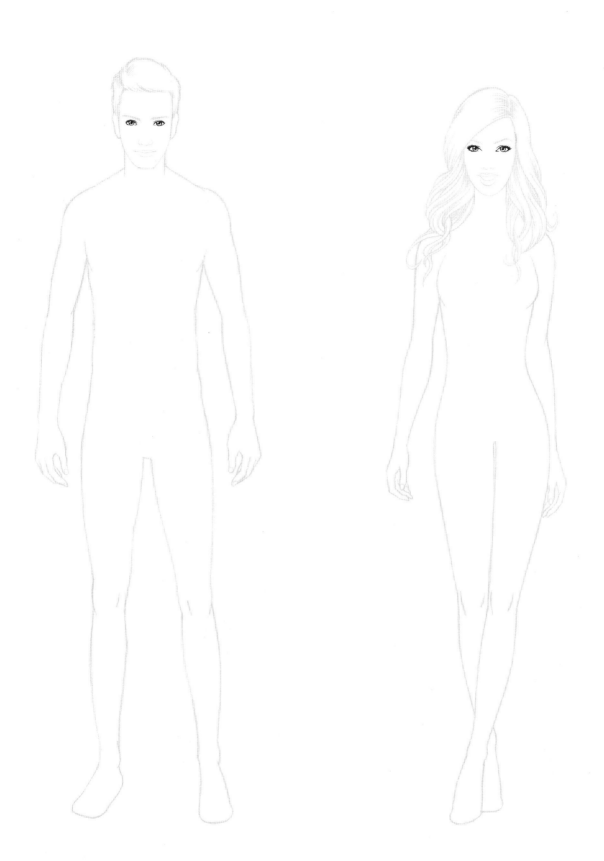

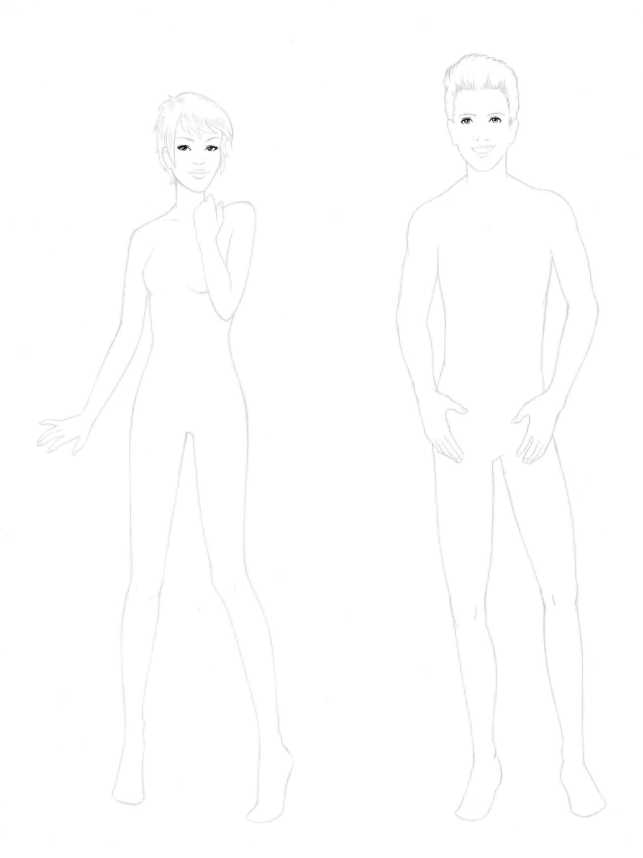

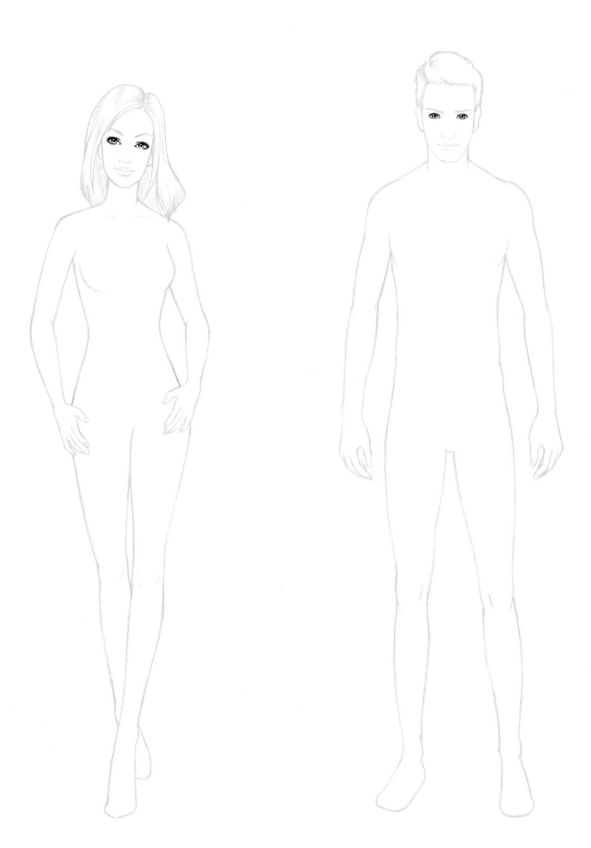

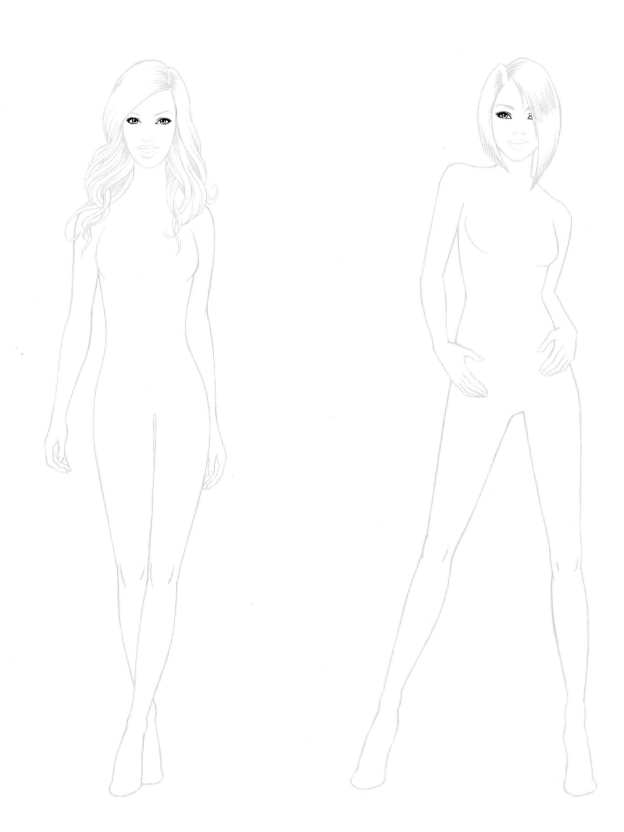

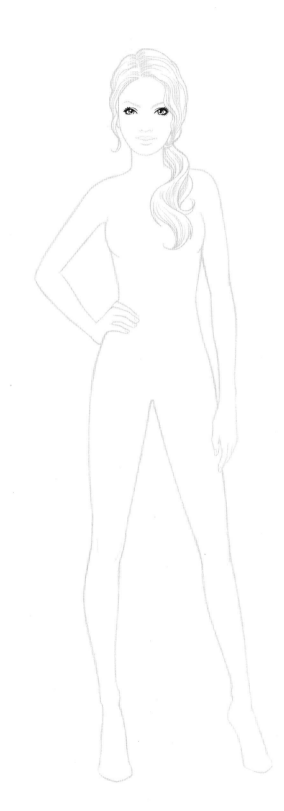

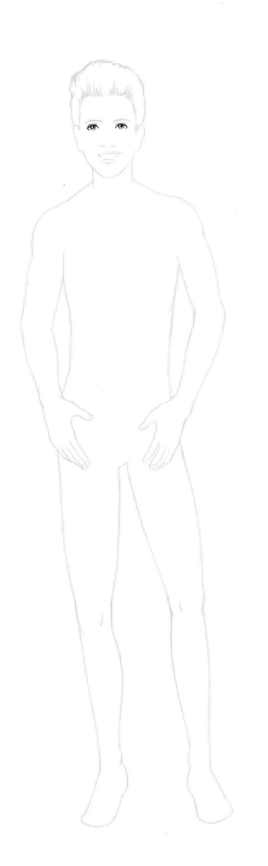

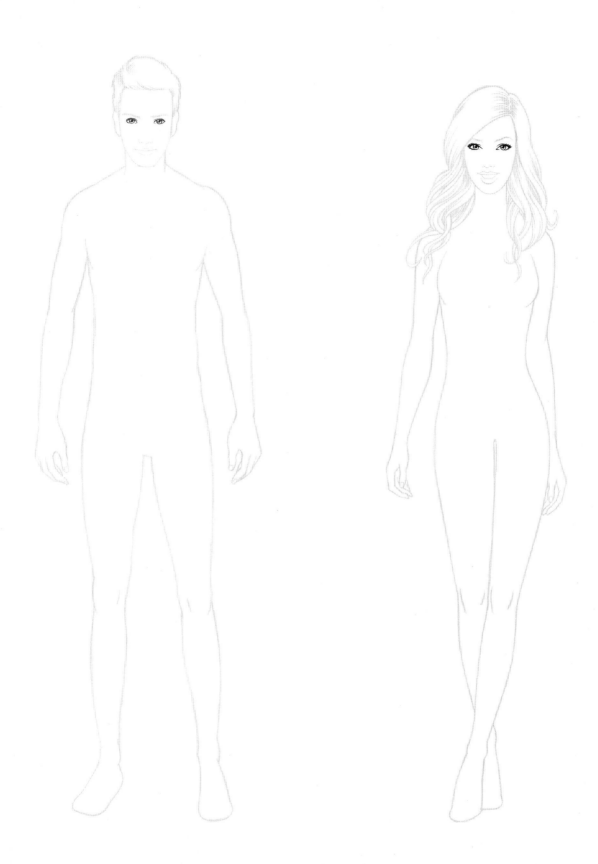

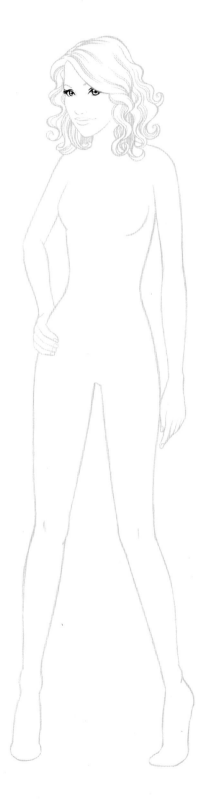